Bertha

and the Lost TOM

Story by **Eric Charles**
Pictures by **Steve Augarde**
from the original television designs by **Ivor Wood**

André Deutsch/Hippo Books

Published simultaneously in hardback by
André Deutsch Limited, 105-106 Great Russell
Street, London WC1B 3LJ and in paperback by
Hippo Books, Scholastic Publications Limited,
10 Earlham Street, London WC2H 9RX in 1987.

ISBN 0 233 97919 0 (hardback)
ISBN 0 590 70466 4 (paperback)

Phototypeset by Kalligraphics Limited,
Redhill, Surrey
Made and printed by Mateu Cromo,
Madrid, Spain

"TOM is getting very clever," said Nell, watching him sort out toy building blocks.

For the past week Bertha, the big machine, had been making coloured building blocks of different shapes and sizes. As they came tumbling down the conveyor belt, TOM picked them out and made them into sets.

"Peep – Peep," he called, as he finished yet another set and sent it down for Nell to pack.

Roy smiled. "TOM only needs a few more wires and circuits to be as clever as you, Ted."

Ted laughed. "It will be a while before that happens – I hope!" He looked at his clipboard and pushed several buttons on the control panel. Bertha's lights flashed and her wheels turned. "CLINK – CLONK – CLANK," she went, and on to the conveyor belt came three round blocks.

Nell shouted over the noise of the machine. "I'm running out of packing boxes, Ted."

Ted pulled the lever and stopped Bertha. He went to the packing table. "Right," he said. "Roy, will you send TOM to Panjid with a note. Say we need more boxes for Bertha."

Roy wrote the note and gave it to TOM. "Take this to Panjid in the dispatch department," he said slowly and clearly, so that TOM would remember the instructions.

The circuits in the robot's memory buzzed and flashed. "Peep – Peep," he said and scooted away, carrying the note.

Nell watched him go. "It's really useful to have a robot for running errands," she chuckled.

Flo was stacking the last of the boxes. "Very useful," she agreed. "I wish we had one at home."

When TOM arrived in the dispatch department, Panjid was moving large wooden crates with the fork-lift truck. TOM gave him the note.

"Just a moment, TOM," Panjid called to him. "I've only got one more box to stack."

The engine roared as he backed the truck. "Watch out!" he shouted as the heavy box swung above the robot's head.

TOM scooted out of the way and stopped by the tool bench. The tools were bright and clean and laid out in tidy rows. There were hammers and screwdrivers, pincers and pliers, a huge wrench and lots of spanners. And there was something else, something that TOM had never seen before. A large magnet, shaped like a horseshoe. TOM reached out and touched it.

"CLONK" went the magnet and attached itself to his metal hand. TOM gave a peep of fright and tried to shake the magnet loose. "PEEEEP – PEEEP!" he cried as he felt its force beginning to upset his sensitive electrical circuits. "PEEEEEEEEP!"

"Hang on, I won't be a minute," shouted Panjid, not knowing why TOM was making such a fuss.

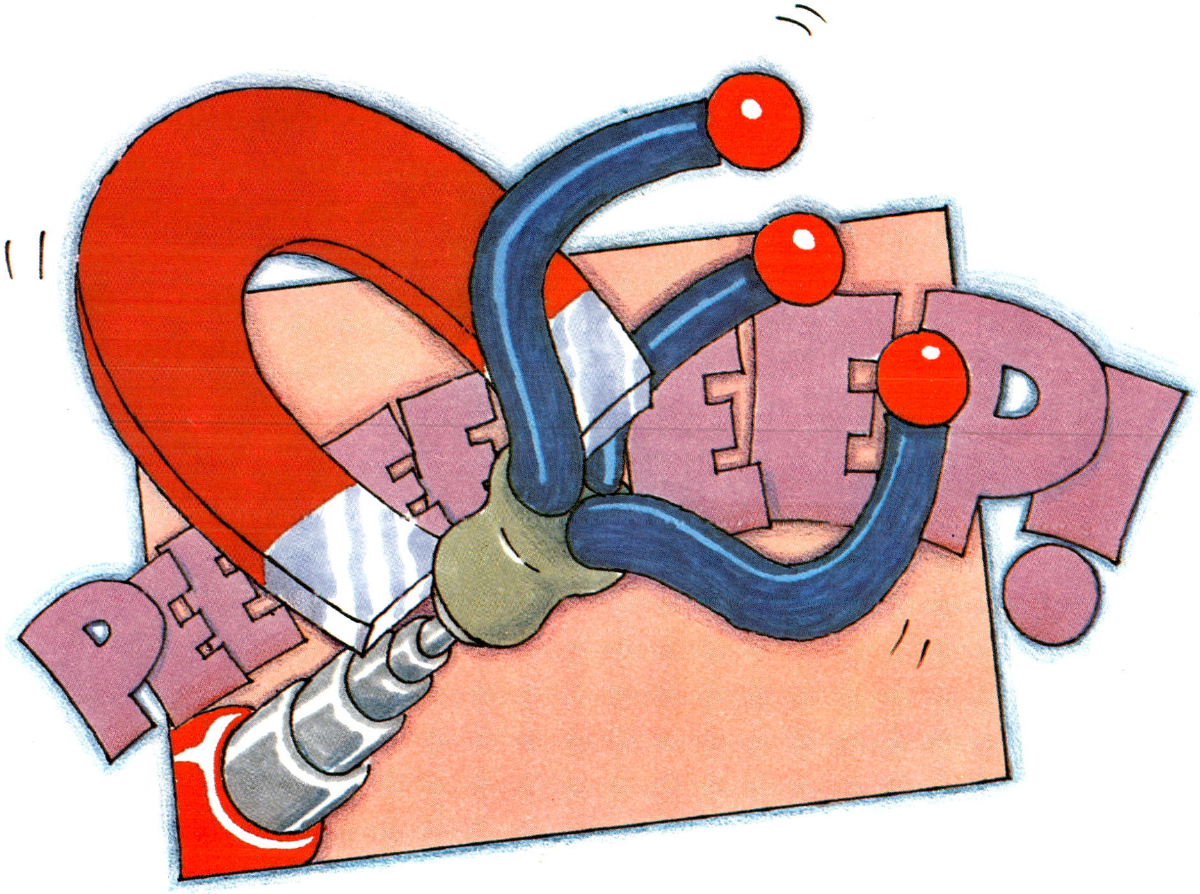

TOM turned in a tight circle, trying to dislodge the magnet, and bumped into the tool bench.

A screwdriver rolled down the wooden top and jumped on to the magnet;

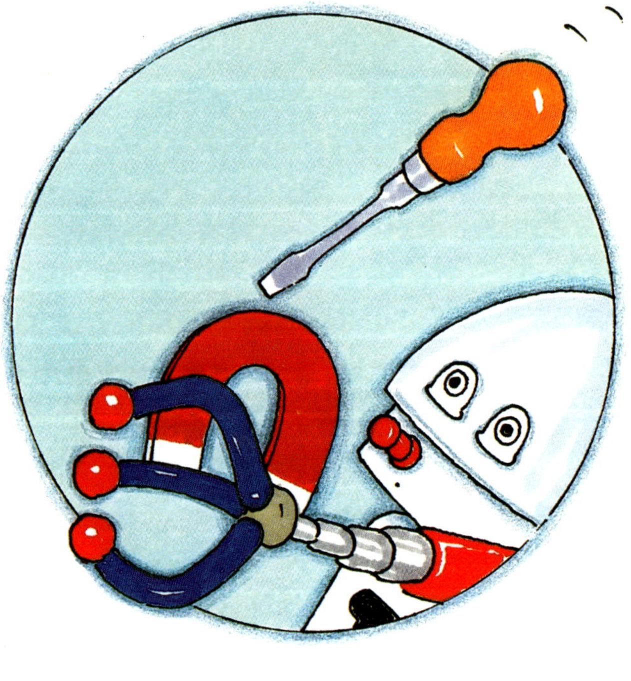

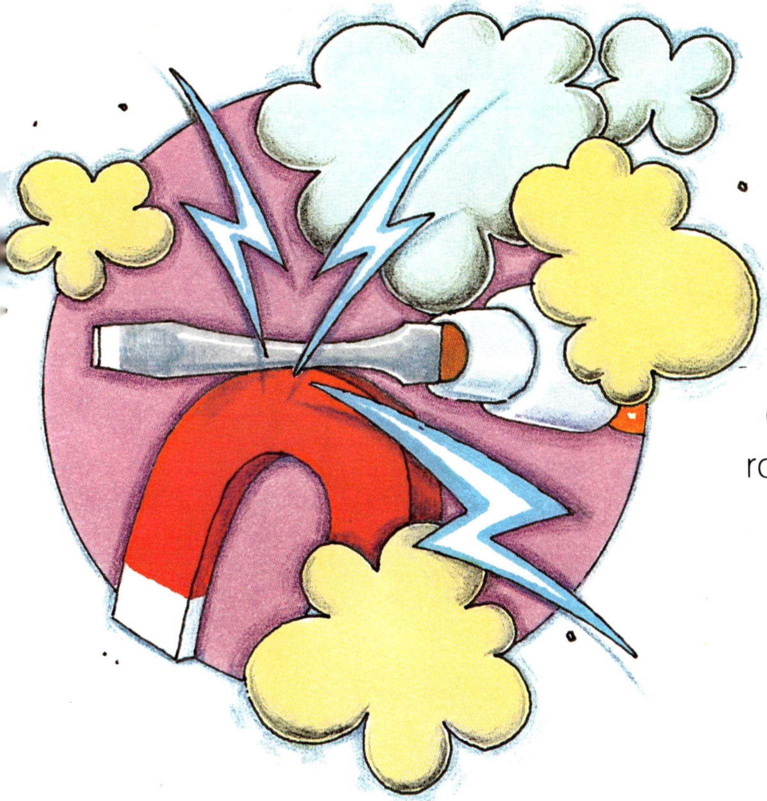

there was a flash of sparks and
a puff of smoke and the little
robot came to a sudden stop.

"Peep – Peeeeeeeep," he cried,
weakly, as his memory faded.

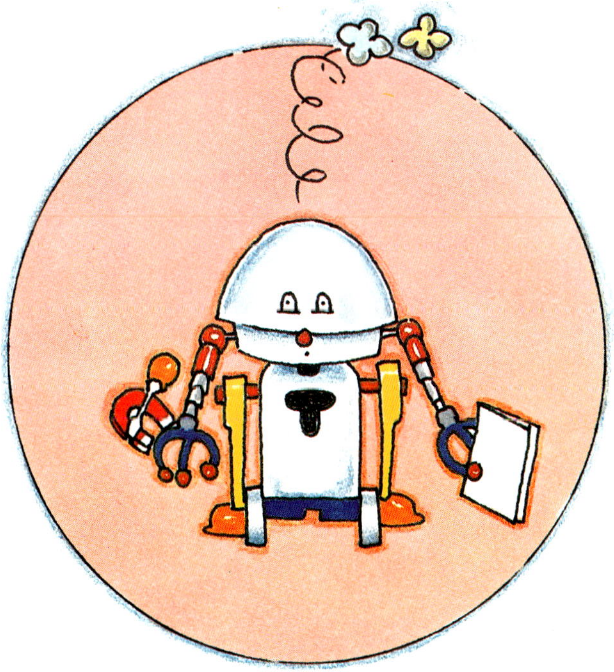

“Tut, tut! All this fuss about a note,” Panjid chided him. He stopped the fork lift truck and took the note. “MORE BOXES FOR BERTHA,” he read. “Well, now, all the new boxes are in the big shed outside. I’ll get some from there and take them over.” He gave the note back to TOM. “I’ll see you there,” he said and drove off.

But TOM no longer remembered the way back to Bertha. He tried going straight ahead, but he bumped into the work bench again; he went backwards and hit the wall with a thump; he turned in a half circle and banged into a packing case. “PEEEP – PEEEEEP!” he wailed, becoming more and more confused.

He turned again, this time to the right and found the way clear. Cautiously he moved forward and found himself in the factory. The noise of the machines was familiar to him, Bertha must be somewhere near. He scooted up the aisle between the machines, turned the corner and bumped into Mr Duncan, the factory foreman.

"Ouch!" cried Mr Duncan, rubbing his knee, "You ought to be more careful, rushing about like that."

TOM offered him the note. "MORE BOXES FOR BERTHA," read Mr Duncan. He scratched his head and pointed to a pile of old boxes lying on the floor. "These are all I've got," he said. "They're rather dirty, but they'll have to do." He gave the note to TOM. "See you at Bertha's," he said, not knowing that TOM was lost, and walked off to find a barrow.

Mrs Tupp was preparing the tea-trolley for the morning break, when TOM came scooting into the kitchen.

"Hello, TOM," she said, "what can I do for you?"

TOM came forward and held out the note.

"A note for me," smiled Mrs Tupp.

She took it and read; MORE BOXES FOR BERTHA. "Goodness me," she said, the only boxes I have are old cake boxes. I'll collect as many as I can and take them down to Bertha. See you there, then," and she handed TOM the note.

TOM wanted her to know that he was lost. "Peep – Peep," he said and moved towards her. He bumped into the tea-trolley. The large urn let out a hiss of steam and a teaspoon rolled off the trolley and attached itself to the magnet. TOM turned and scooted out of the kitchen.

Back with Bertha, Ted was still waiting for boxes and wondering what had happened to TOM.

"He should have been here ages ago," said Roy.

"Well, he can't have got lost between here and the dispatch department," said Nell.

"He'll be back soon," said Flo. "He can't be far away."

But TOM was far away.

Miss McClackerty was in her office, typing, when she heard a strange peeping sound coming from outside her door. When she opened it she was surprised to see little TOM scoot past her into the office.

"Hello, TOM," she said, "What are you doing here?" TOM offered her the note. MORE BOXES FOR BERTHA, she read. "I don't know why they've sent you here," she said, "the only boxes that I have are full of envelopes. Oh well, I'll tip the envelopes out and take the empty boxes down to Bertha." Miss McClackerty sat down at her desk, folded the note and gave it back to TOM. "Thank you for bringing it," she said.

As TOM took the note, all the paper clips on the desk were attracted to the magnet. "PING – CLINK, PING – CLINK," they went as they attached themselves to it. Before Miss McClackerty could say a word, TOM turned and scooted out of the office.

Further along the corridor, in the design office, Mr Spott and Tracy were working on a new type of toy building block. "If I can find a way to make these blocks hold together, it will be a lot more fun building with them," said Mr Sprott.

Tracy heard a noise. "Is that your watch, peeping, Mr Sprott?" she asked.

"No," said Mr Sprott, "my watch doesn't peep!"

They both listened. The peeping sound came again. "Perhaps it's your computer," Mr Sprott said.

"No. My computer doesn't make that sort of noise," said Tracy. She opened the office door. TOM rushed past her, waving the note.

"Well, well," laughed Mr Sprott, "it's your robot friend with a note."

When Mr Sprott read it he shook his head. "MORE BOXES FOR BERTHA?" he said. "*We* haven't any boxes. I wonder why Ted sent him here?"

Tracy looked closely at TOM. "I think there is something wrong with him," she said. "I don't think he was sent here at all. He looks as if he's lost."

"Lost?" Mr Sprott said, surprised. "How do robots get themselves lost?"

"PEEEP – PEEEEP," cried TOM and held out his hand.
"Ah! I see what's the matter," said Tracy, removing the magnet from TOM's hand. "This has upset his senstive electronic circuits." She handed the magnet to Mr Sprott.

“Just look at the things it has collected.” Mr Sprott held up the screwdriver, teaspoon and paper clips. “TOM must have been all over the factory.”

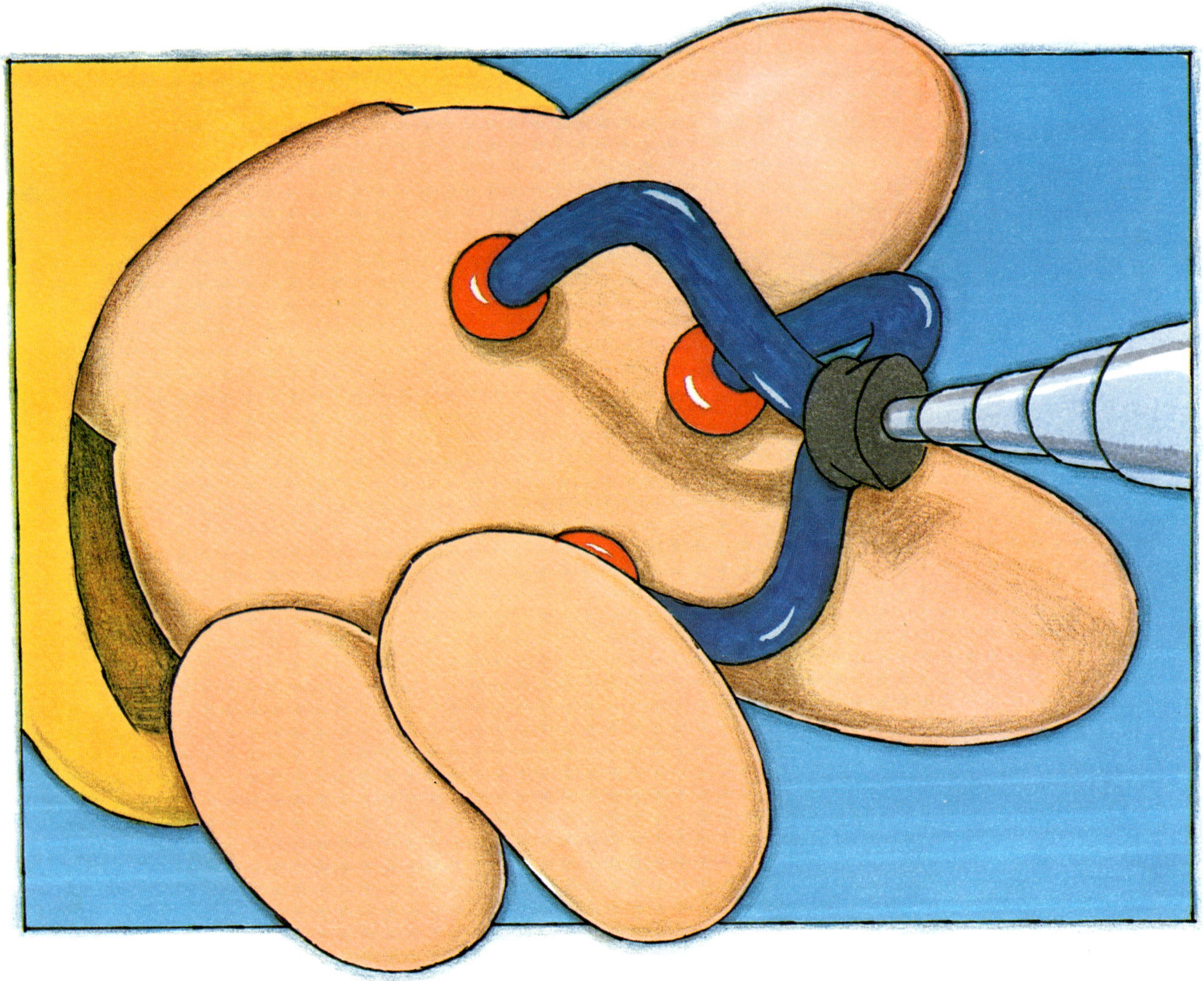

Tracy smiled at the little robot. “You’ve had a busy morning,” she said.

“Peep – Peep,” agreed TOM. Now that the magnet had been removed his memory was coming back and he was beginning to feel much better.

Tracy took him by the hand. “I’ll take you over to Bertha,” she said and led him out of the office.

Mr Sprott looked thoughtfully at the magnet. "If small magnets were put inside building blocks, they would stick together!" he murmured, and hurried to his drawing board.

When Tracy and TOM got back to Bertha, there was a mountain of boxes piled up around her. There were dirty old boxes brought by Mr Duncan, cake boxes from Mrs Tupp's kitchen, empty envelope boxes that Miss McClackerty had carried down from the office, all mixed up with the new ones that Panjid had fetched from the big shed outside.

When Ted saw TOM approaching, he shook his head and smiled. "Here comes the busy little robot that has caused all the trouble," he chuckled, "I reckon he must have been round the whole factory asking for boxes."

"Very nearly," said Tracy and she explained about the magnet upsetting TOM's memory.

"So that's what happened," said Ted, "I thought something must have gone wrong."

"Fancy that," said Flo.

"Poor TOM couldn't help it," said Nell.

"I don't care what was to blame," said Roy, "I'm just glad he's back."

Mr Sprott came hurrying down from the design office and gave Ted the plans for the new building blocks. "TOM gave me the idea for the magnets," he said, "do you think Bertha can make them?"

"Bertha can make anything," said Ted, giving his big machine a pat.

"CLINK – CLONK," agreed Bertha.

"Just watch out that TOM doesn't touch any of those magnets," said Tracy, "he's been lost enough for one day."

"PEEP – PEEEP," said TOM and he turned in a tight circle, glad to be back with Bertha and his workmates.